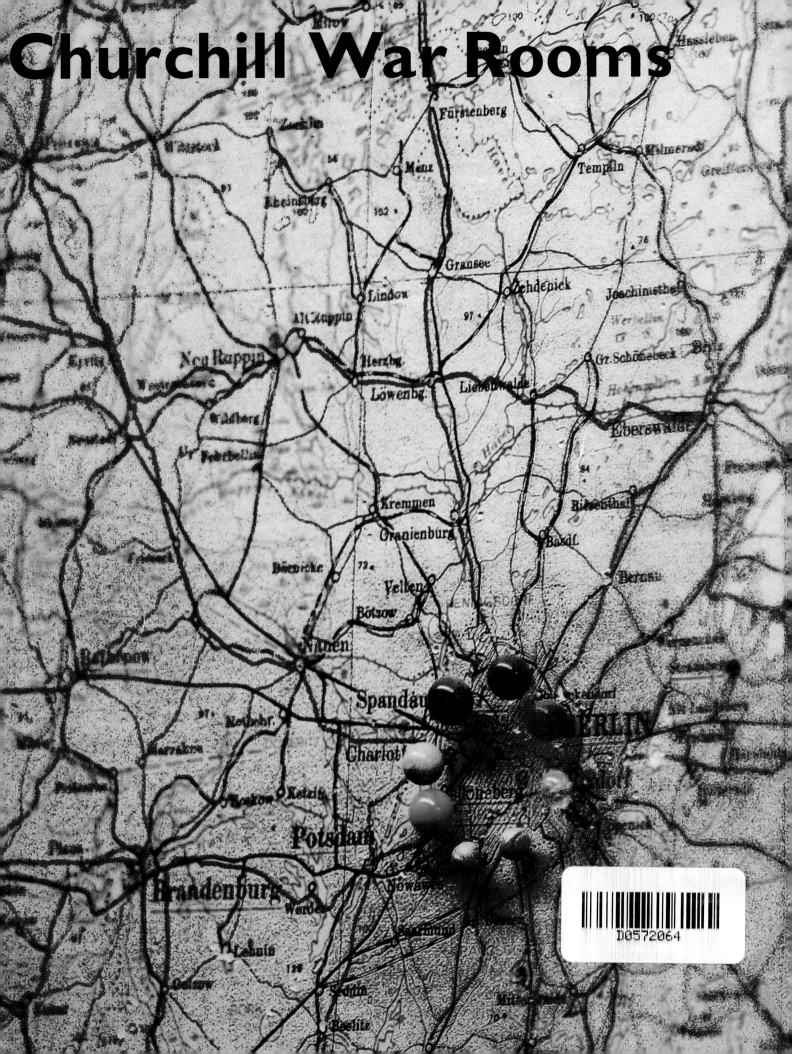

# Churchill War Rooms

Welcome to Churchill War Rooms, one of the five branches of IWM (Imperial War Museums).

The Rooms first became operational at the end of August 1939, but only really came into their own after Winston Churchill became Prime Minister and it is with him that they will forever be associated. The War Cabinet Room was the scene of numerous crucial meetings held by Churchill during the Blitz, as, above ground, the Luftwaffe tried to devastate London. It was in his subterranean room that Churchill contemplated the route of a possible Nazi invasion, and it was to the adjacent Map Room that he brought his most important visitors to demonstrate its high-tech, intense, but calm charting of the war.

In the late 1970s the Imperial War Museum was tasked with preserving the historic site and contents of the Cabinet War Rooms, and making them known and accessible to as wide an audience as possible. Today the Rooms enjoy a worldwide reputation as a unique historic site, and also as the location of the award-winning Churchill Museum. As you walk through the Rooms today, you step back into history and breathe in the atmosphere of those times, the air still redolent of the smells and sounds of daily – and nightly – life there.

Witnesses from those times are now rare and it is left to us to preserve their memories, their experiences and, in the case of the War Rooms, their very working environment. In 2005 we added the only major museum in the world dedicated to the life and legacy of Sir Winston Churchill. The Churchill Museum was opened by Her Majesty The Queen, and awarded the Council of Europe Museums Award the following year. Its multimedia and uniquely engaging approach to display continues to fascinate visitors of all ages.

I hope that this guide will provide happy memories of a very enjoyable visit and will encourage you to make further visits to this and other branches of IWM, described on the final page. IWM relies greatly on the support of the Friends of the Imperial War Museum and our many teams of volunteers, as well as those who support us with donations and legacies. If you would like to help us, please visit our website for further details, **iwm.org.uk.**

**Diane Lees, Director-General
IWM**

Winston Churchill has long been a source of inspiration to a remarkable cast of statesmen and women of diverse political convictions from all corners of the globe. General de Gaulle described him as 'the great artist of a great history', while President Johnson saw in him 'the greatest of all American citizens' (Churchill was made an honorary citizen of the United States by President Kennedy in 1963). Though Churchill was a lifelong opponent of Communism, his admirers include the former Prime Minister of Russia, Mr Chernomyrdin, and the leader of the Cuban revolution, Fidel Castro. Visitors to the War Cabinet Room include many illustrious names: US Presidents Clinton and George W Bush, President Sarkozy, Chairman Yasser Arafat, Prime Minister Benjamin Netanyahu, Presidents and Prime Ministers from Japan, Albania, Croatia, Australia and many, many more.

Nowhere captures the indefatigable spirit and steadfast resolution with which Sir Winston Churchill is identified more than this scene of his 'finest hour'. They are kept today as they were when he last worked here with his Ministers, Chiefs of Staff and a vast support staff, whose more humble accommodations recall their labours and the long hours spent below ground. To generations who lived through those times, as much as generations for whom the Second World War is distant history, Churchill War Rooms brings alive the experiences of both the nation's leaders and those who served anonymously through the uncertainty of 1940 to the relief and rejoicing of 1945.

The museum we have established here in Churchill's name focuses on the story of the Rooms' most famous occupant, enabling visitors to go behind the familiar images and instantly recognisable phrases of his best-known oratory, and to understand how Churchill came to hold the position he now does in the minds and hearts of people all around the world.

Churchill War Rooms offers an enjoyable and engaging means of learning about historic times and historic figures in a unique historic setting, the memory of which will linger on.

**Phil Reed, Director
Churchill War Rooms**

# 'I felt as if I were walking with destiny and that all my past life had been but a preparation for this hour and this trial'

**Winston Churchill**

As the 1930s advanced and another conflict on the scale of the 'Great War' became more likely, military planners began to prepare for the expected air war. By this time bomber aircraft had been developed to a point that aerial bombardment of cities – which had been an ever more common feature of the First World War – was expected to be both a frequent and devastating occurrence. The decision had been taken in 1938 to establish a central emergency working refuge for the War Cabinet and the Chiefs of Staff as a safeguard against a sudden air attack. The resulting 'Cabinet War Rooms', the British government's secret underground shelter, became fully operational on Sunday 27 August 1939, one week before the outbreak of the Second World War.

Basement storage rooms under the Office of Works and the Board of Trade in the 'New Public Offices' were chosen for their central position and for the uncommonly strong structure of the building above them. Developed as a short-term measure, the accommodation was basic and without frills, indeed without many everyday services. This temporary solution was to become home to a host of civil servants and military personnel and the frequent shelter of government ministers, including the Prime Minister, Winston Churchill himself, for the next six years.

**Below Blackboard showing the tally of aircraft believed to have been shot down on 'Battle of Britain Day', 15 September 1940.
Opposite On 31 July 1940 Churchill inspected coastal fortifications and defence works. He is seen here on a sandbagged gun emplacement with its defenders.**

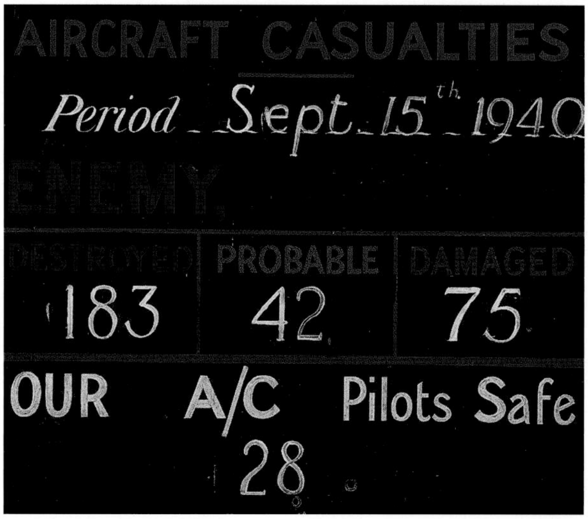

AIRCRAFT CASUALTIES
Period Sept. 15th 1940
ENEMY

| DESTROYED | PROBABLE | DAMAGED |
|-----------|----------|---------|
| 183 | 42 | 75 |

OUR    A/C    Pilots Safe
28

# Cabinet War Rooms

# War Cabinet Room

## 'This is the room from which I will lead the war'

Winston Churchill, shortly after being appointed Prime Minister on 10 May 1940

## How did people access the CWR?

The front door through which visitors enter today did not exist during the Second World War. Most people entered through the building above by the entrance opposite St James's Park, (now The Treasury Building). The flight of steps into the building, then further steps inside and the descent into the CWR via the gloomy 'Staircase 15' seems to have given many people the impression of being deeper underground than they actually were. Churchill used the same route. His upstairs HQ, 'Number 10 Annexe', was situated on the ground floor facing the park.

Churchill disliked his underground shelter, and the War Cabinet met in this room only when the bombing raids made meeting on the surface an unacceptable risk. Despite the measures taken to protect him, he sometimes took himself – and occasional visitors – onto the roof of the building above to watch the air raids in progress.

The room which gave the site its name was chosen simply because it was the biggest available. The humble Civil Service furnishings and the overcrowded layout betray the planned temporary nature of the room.

Apart from the absence of a constant fug of cigar and cigarette smoke, the scene in the room has changed little in the years since it closed at the end of the war in 1945. It is today just as the wartime occupants experienced it during the 115 meetings of the War Cabinet, which took place in this room, and during the copious meetings of the Defence Committee under the chairmanship of Winston Churchill. The same maps decorate the room now as then.

Momentous decisions were taken in this room and the scratched arms of the seat in which Churchill sat bear witness to the tensions of those crucial meetings at critical moments of the war.

# Transatlantic
# Telephone Room

**Why are all the clocks stopped at 5 o'clock?**
For convenience! Most of them do not work and those that do need regular up-dating and winding. The time of 5pm was chosen for all the clocks and marks the beginning of the War Cabinet meeting on 15 October 1940, the day after bombs severely damaged Number 10 Downing Street, which finally persuaded Churchill to meet in the CWR on a regular basis.

The Transatlantic telephone cable was not laid until after the war and, until then, telephone communications between the UK and the USA were via a radio–telephone link. During the war access to this link was very strictly controlled and secrecy was monitored by a civilian at either end, who listened in to the conversation. If Mr Churchill or President Roosevelt said anything which secrecy forbad them mentioning, the line would be cut and they would be (warily) advised not to mention the subject.

In 1943 Bell Telephones brought their latest scrambler device, Sigsaly, to London, having installed one in the Pentagon. It was intended for, and used by, the top US military in London and, through its sophisticated electronics, made the signal almost impenetrable to an enemy. The 40 tons of equipment that made up Sigsaly was installed in the basement of Selfridges Department store in Oxford Street.

In order to ensure that conversations between the Prime Minister and the US President could be conducted in greater security, an extension was installed at the Cabinet War Rooms in the summer of 1943. Legend has it that the President and Churchill were both reluctant to come to the phone until the other was on the line. The British method of disguising the top secret function of the room was to install a toilet lock on the door – resulting, so it is said, in staff believing the room contained the only proper toilet, which would inevitably be the PM's!

**Opposite** The scrambler for Churchill's Cabinet War Rooms transatlantic telephone connection. Known as 'Sigsaly', the equipment was so large it was housed in Selfridge's basement in Oxford Street.
**Above** Clock in the Map Room, with the V (for victory) highlighted by a member of staff.
**Left** The Transatlantic Telephone room as it can be seen today.

**How safe were the Cabinet War Rooms?**
As a converted basement, not a purpose-built bunker, protection was not guaranteed. Even after the installation of the concrete slab over much of the site at Churchill's insistence, the building could well have collapsed if it received a direct hit by a large bomb. There were also fears of flooding, poison gas attack, and infiltration by enemy spies or parachutists. Secrecy was the site's best defence.

The exhibition *Undercover: Life in Churchill's Bunker* explores the stories of some of the hundreds of staff who worked in the Cabinet War Rooms through their personal objects, oral histories and specially made film interviews. A huge administrative staff was required to run the Rooms, including shorthand typists, clerks, and telephonists, not to mention the military policemen and Royal Marine orderlies who helped guard the site (and in the latter case also carried out domestic tasks). Pressure on the staff was great, but for many the work was fascinating and all were aware of its importance to the war effort. Surviving documents and accounts show how the staff shared clothing coupons and jokes, and formed lifelong friendships.

The exhibition also looks at their relationships with Churchill, which varied greatly according to position: some staff worked very closely with him at the Cabinet War Rooms, others were only allowed into restricted areas but glimpsed the Premier in the corridors. A privileged group of Cabinet War Rooms staff were chosen to accompany Churchill to the overseas international war conferences. These conferences were hard work but gave the chosen staff access to unrationed food and a welcome extra clothing allowance.

**Above** Gas mask adapted so that switchboard operators could continue their work even under gas attack. Poisonous gas attack, as practised during the First World War, was greatly feared but never occurred.
**Left** Cabinet War Rooms shorthand typist Ilene Hutchinson, one of the administrative team who accompanied Churchill to the Yalta Conference.
**Opposite** The exhibition *Undercover: Life in Churchill's Bunker*

# Undercover

"A SMALL, VERY CLOSELY-KNIT AND INFORMAL OFFICE, WITH NO PROTOCOL AND ALL THAT SORT OF NONSENSE AND, I THINK, HIGHLY EFFICIENT"

BRIGADIER SIR IAN JACOB ON THE MILITARY SECTION OF THE SECRETARIAT

## EDWARD BRIDGES

## OLIVE CHRISTOPHER

## DENNIS WHEATLEY

## EDWARD KING-SALTER

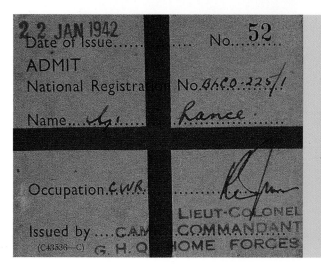

2 2 JAN 1942
Date of Issue...... ..... No...52...

ADMIT

National Registration No.AACO-225/1

Name...Mr..... Rance.......

Occupation.C.W.R. ..........

Issued by ....CAMP COMMANDANT
(C43536—C) G.H.Q. HOME FORCES
LIEUT-COLONEL

**Did the Nazis know about the CWR?**
The captured files which the SS prepared for
their special units to investigate people and
institutions after the invasion of England are
held at IWM London. Nowhere is the CWR,
a converted storage basement, only yards
from Number 10 Downing Street, mentioned.

**Left** Mr George Rance's
Cabinet War Rooms pass.
**Below** Mrs Churchill's
room as photographed in
1946.
**Opposite** The Churchills'
kitchen in the Churchill
Suite.

In 1941 the Cabinet War Rooms expanded into
an area known as the Courtyard Rooms. Here a
series of study bedrooms were created for
Churchill's private office staff, a bedroom for his
wife Clementine and a dining room for them both.
By the time the rooms were prepared, the worst
of the bombing raids had passed and, though they
were fully maintained, they seem to have been
infrequently used.

Photographs taken shortly after the war show
what the rooms looked like. These helped us to
restore them. When we finally took them over in
2001, they were in a very sorry state after years of
neglect and abuse. While the restoration cannot
match every single detail of the original, every
effort was taken to restore their original appearance,
particularly in respect of the two matching 1930s
Jackson electric stoves and the pans handed down
from Churchill's cook, Mrs Landemare, to her
granddaughter.

Winston Churchill liked to have his wife near him
and when he moved his HQ to the ground floor
of the building, immediately above his CWR
bunker, a room was set aside for Clementine next
door to his own. The Churchills were devoted to
each other and, throughout their long and happy
marriage, Clementine was his adviser and confidante
and Churchill regularly shared state secrets with her.

Churchill Suite

# Rooms 59–63

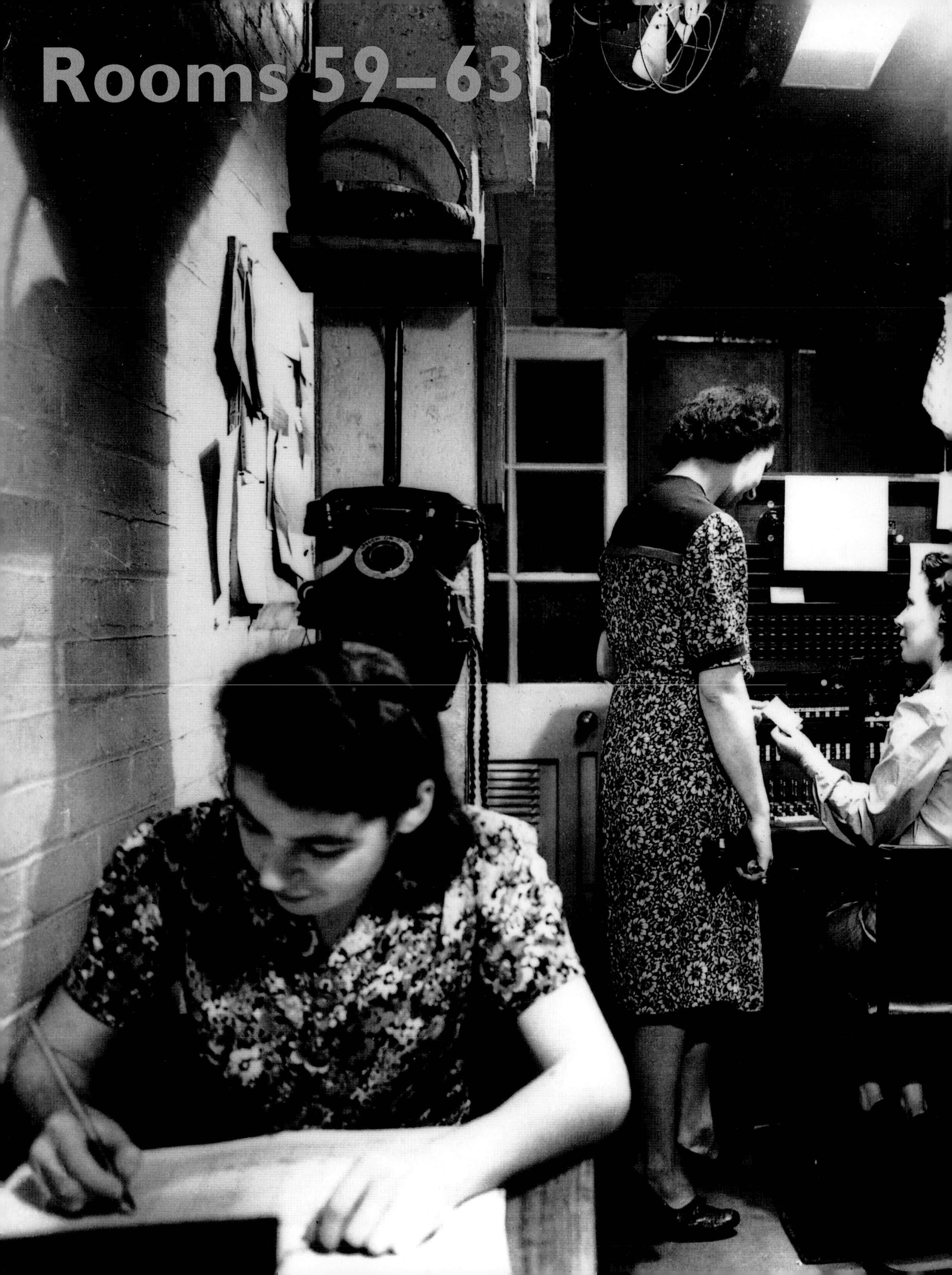

### Where did people eat?

The Shop is situated in what was the officers' mess. The mess contained basic cooking facilities and supplies. Others were fed from supplies in the sub-basement, which had enough food to sustain the site for only a matter of days in case of an emergency. Most of the CWR staff went to their regular shops and cafés on the surface.

The uses of the various rooms in the Cabinet War Rooms altered to respond to the changing demands of war. When the Imperial War Museum reinstated them in the early 1980s it was decided to restore the service rooms to the same appearance and purpose of 1940. At that time the principal demands were for accommodation for the Joint Planning Staff, who undertook the essential work of operational planning, and for Home Forces, whose presence close to the Chiefs of Staff and Churchill became vital as invasion from Hitler's forces seemed imminent. Administrative support for Churchill was provided by the Cabinet Office, and the senior staff of this body also needed to be close at hand. The result was severe pressure on space. The Joint Planning Staff were pressed into Room 59, their typing services into 60A, Home Defence – in a graduation from junior staff officers to the Commander in Chief – took over Rooms 62, 62A and 62B respectively. The Cabinet Secretary, Sir Edward Bridges, and his military equivalent, General Ismay (who also served as Churchill's personal Chief of Staff) were given rooms which doubled up as bedrooms and offices, alongside their private secretaries in partitioned Rooms 61 Left and Right and 61A Left and Right.

Communications were always high on the list of priorities and concerns. In Room 60 the BBC set up broadcasting equipment which allowed the Prime Minister to broadcast on four occasions to the UK, Europe and the United States. A single unit telephone switchboard was installed in Room 60, but, as demand outgrew the resource, it was superseded by a five operator unit installed in the room which now serves as the Switchroom Café.

# The Map Room

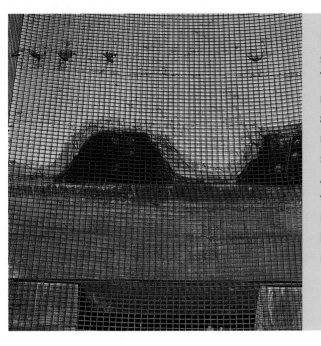

**How thick was the concrete detonator slab and how did they install it?**
The techniques used for installing such massive and numerous steel support girders and the steel waffle containment are a mystery. They were installed, without arousing suspicion and into an existing building, using American supplied concrete pumps. Until the first two-metre deep section was put in place in December 1940, three months into the heavy bombing raids, the CWR had virtually no protection against aerial bombardment.

Staffed by one officer each of the Royal Air Force, the Army and the Royal Navy, twenty-four hours every day, from August 1939 to August 1945, the principal function of the Map Room was to act as an around-the-clock central point for information about the war. Each day by 8am the Map Room officers produced a daily summary of the war for the King, the Prime Minister and the Chiefs of Staff.

The room has scarcely changed from its appearance as shown in photographs taken towards the end of the war: the so-called 'beauty chorus' of colour-coded direct line telephones; the flickering strip lights; the rare air conditioning unit; the books and documents littering the tables – all has remained as the Map Room staff left it when the lights were finally extinguished on 16 August 1945.

The wartime maps still cover the walls. The wall-length chart is punctuated by tens of thousands of tiny holes showing the hazardous voyages of the naval convoys. Maps of Java, Thailand and the Pacific theatre show the front lines as they were just before the end of the war in the Far East. In the Map Room Annexe the wall is covered by a map of the great land mass of Russia, its original coloured pins and cotton showing the front line from 1941 to the fall of Berlin in 1945.

The Map Room also contains two very human elements. On the desk of the Chief Map Room Officer is an envelope marked with his name and the rationed sugar cubes that he hid in it, which lay forgotten in his drawer until found in 1980. And the blackboard is permanently painted with the date of 15 September 1940 – the day on which the Battle of Britain turned in Britain 's favour. This reminds us how crucial the battle for air supremacy was in preventing Hitler from safely transporting his troops across the English Channel and, in effect, marking the turning point of the war.

**Opposite The Map Room as it can be seen today. Above The two-metre thick 'slab' revealed. Below Map pins box. Overleaf Close-up of the Convoy Map in the Map Room, heavily punctuated and worn away by pins marking convoy movements.**

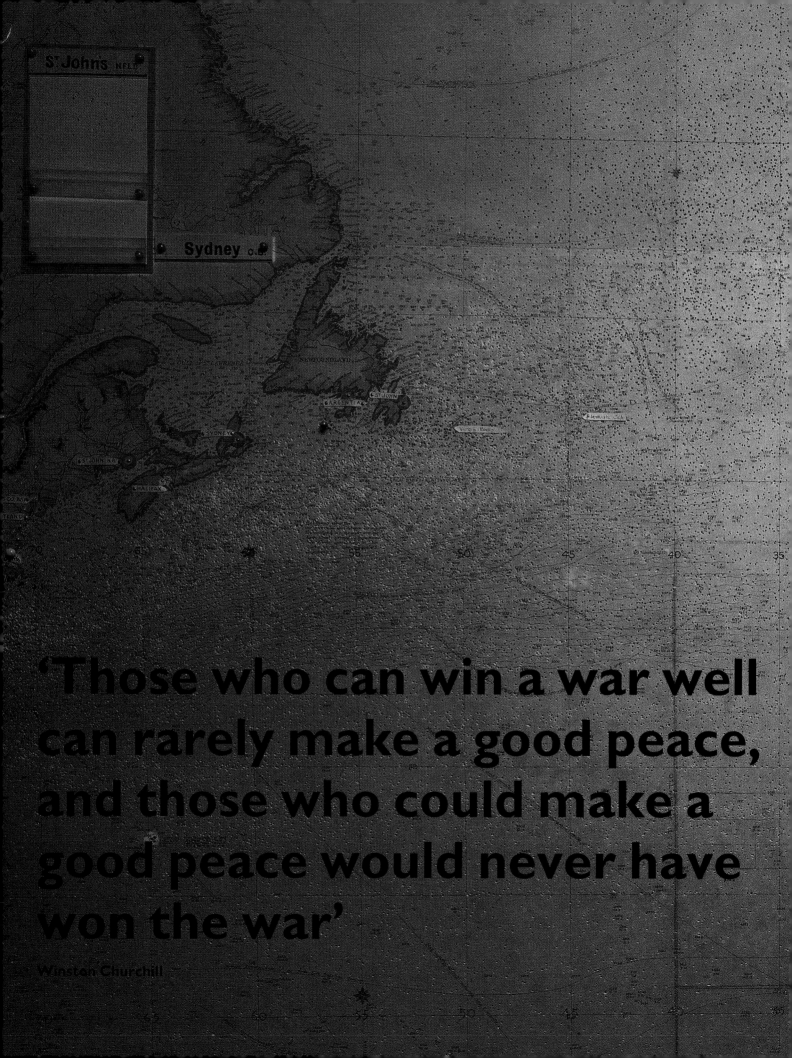

'Those who can win a war well can rarely make a good peace, and those who could make a good peace would never have won the war'

Winston Churchill

**Was there a tunnel connecting the CWR to Downing Street?**
Officials deny the existence of such tunnels but this has not dampened widespread speculation that they exist. In any event, Churchill seems to have reached the building by car or on foot.

This room was kept throughout the war as it looks today, though the Prime Minister only used it as a bedroom on three occasions. In 1940 he preferred to use the Railway Board Executive's more comfortably equipped conversion of a disused Tube station at Down Street, where he could enjoy his habit of two baths a day, a proper toilet system and a good stock of fine wines.

He used his room at the CWR for visits to the Map Room and for business when forced to meet underground. He also delivered four of his wartime speeches from here, including his 11 September 1940 speech, warning of Hitler's plans to wage a war of terror against the United Kingdom. Mrs Churchill also broadcast ten speeches to Russian listeners on behalf of the 'Red Cross Aid to Russia' charity.

The room boasts wall-to-wall carpet, but only a small standard Civil Service bed. The 'ash tray' is a suitably large metal canister into which Churchill could throw his cigar stubs, while one wall is covered by maps showing possible landing grounds for Hitler's armies, reflecting Churchill's constant concern in 1940.

In December 1940 conversion of the ground floor rooms of the building above was complete. These came to be known as the 'Number 10 Annexe', and it was here that Churchill lived and worked until his defeat in the July 1945 General Election.

**Left** The Prime Minister's bed with emergency lighting close at hand. **Above** Churchill leaves for Parliament on the morning of 6 June 1944, to announce the Allied landings in France. **Opposite** Churchill's desk in his office-bedroom. The microphones were provided by the BBC for his broadcasts to the outside world.

# Churchill's Room

PW/LR
5004

SPEECH

To War Office
War Room

# TELEPHONES

| TADWORTH 3186 | FIRE POST Room 52 269 | A.I.3.(b). AM 2 |
| SLOANE 2208 | RUSBATCH 5205 | P.R.2. 5166 |
| BEACONSFIELD 911 | | C.S.U |
| HAMPSTEAD 2217 | FIRST AID POST 5019 | RAID ASSESSMENT |
| EMBERBROOK 1840 | | CASUALTIES HOLBORN 3434 EXT 663 |
| UPLANDS 6186 | M.O. 5019 5815 | AMWIS AM 2 |
| FRETWELL WES 676 | RAF DORMITORY (61A) 674 | DAVIS. A.M.W.R. 5001 |
| GROSVENOR 1209 | | |

## What were conditions in the CWR like?

Probably the worst aspect of life in the CWR was the lack of proper toilet facilities. When the site was adapted in 1938, no system for the automatic removal of sewage was installed. This meant that chemical toilets, known as Elsans, had to be used, making the sub-basement in particular somewhat smelly. Washing facilities generally consisted of bowls and buckets; the sub-basement, where most people had sleeping spaces, was very inhospitable. Conditions were cramped and vermin, cigarette smoke and the noise of the air supply system added to the unpleasant atmosphere. Working hours tended to be 'flexible' and if the job required you to stay hours beyond the end of your shift, you stayed. Being underground for long periods of daylight created the risk of vitamin D deficiency and arrangements were made for the typists and others to be given sunlamp treatment to lessen the risk. Keeping a secret was not difficult; you did not pry into offices which were nothing to do with you and you didn't ask questions. If anyone did ask too many, they were reported and would probably be 're-posted'.

The War Cabinet met in the Cabinet War Rooms for the last time on 28 March 1945, when the last V-weapon fell on Greater London. The Map Room and the Cabinet War Rooms formally ceased functioning on 16 August 1945. The administrative rooms were stripped of their contents and returned to storage and service areas. The Office of Works representative, Mr Rance, stayed on and acted as occasional guide to the Cabinet Room, the Map Room, Churchill's Room and the Transatlantic Telephone Room, which had been left intact. In 1948 the government formally undertook to preserve these rooms and, following widespread publicity, guided tours were arranged. In 1984, the Imperial War Museum finished its project to restore the site and opened it to the public. Churchill War Rooms has been a branch of the Imperial War Museum since 1989.

In 2001 work began to restore those areas which had not been accessible to the public in 1984, and the Learning and Conference Centre was opened as part of this in 2003. The final element of the restoration project, the Churchill Museum, opened in 2005.

Churchill War Rooms receives no direct government subsidy and the 2002–2005 work on restoration was carried out as a result of the generosity of a wide range of people and organisations across the world and the National Heritage Memorial Fund. We are extremely grateful to all our supporters for their help in ensuring the permanent preservation of this unique historic site and for their help in establishing the Churchill Museum.

**Opposite** One of the colourful array of telephones, nicknamed 'the beauty chorus' by those who worked in the Map Room.
**Above** A member of the Cabinet War Rooms staff updates the weather indicator.
**Below** Detail of the original emergency exit signage.

Churchill Museum

# 'We are all worms, but I do believe that I am a glow-worm'

**Winston Churchill**

To some degree the man widely acknowledged as Britain's greatest politician and historical figure, Winston Churchill, has become a two dimensional and slightly unreal character. His reputation rests largely on superficial knowledge, constantly replayed images and on one brief – albeit momentous – period of his life. The Churchill Museum has taken on a difficult task: a 'personality museum' could so easily slip in the pitfalls of dullness or hagiography. There was a clear need for a museum which could explore the complex nature of Churchill's life and his long political career; a museum which would not have as its purpose either revisionism, iconoclasm or hero worship; a museum which would tell the story in revealing and truthful detail, would show aspects of his life and personality which were unknown or forgotten; a museum which, overall, would explain and illustrate why his reputation is as high as it is, how he achieved that reputation and, of course, why he merits a museum in his name.

Using cutting edge technology and a mixture of display media, the undeniably exciting story of a major figure in British and world history is brought to life. And that story begins at the moment which is the most familiar of its long course: 10 May 1940, Churchill's appointment as Prime Minister.

**Opposite** Photograph of Winston Churchill by Yousuf Karsh, which looks over the Lifeline table. **Above** Entrance to the Churchill Museum. **Below left** Churchill on the day he became Prime Minister, 10 May 1940.

# Young Churchill

To fully understand Winston Churchill it is necessary to understand his heritage and upbringing. These put him on the path he was to follow and gave him the characteristics which virtually became his trademark.

Churchill was born at Blenheim Palace, the home of his grandfather the Duke of Marlborough, on 30 November 1874. His father, whom he idolised, was the eminent politician – though soon to fall from favour – Lord Randolph Churchill. His mother, whom he adored, was the beautiful American heiress, Jennie Jerome. Despite his loving admiration for his parents, their attitude to Winston was marked by a neglect that was typical of the social mores of high society at that time. His regular pleas for his parents to visit him at school went largely ignored and his emotional needs were only met by his beloved nanny, Mrs Everest.

Churchill's schooling at Harrow was marked by adventure and limited academic achievement, though he already showed skill in recitation which would serve him well in his later career. His father, scornful of his school record, pressed him towards a military career, which the young Churchill pursued with vigour and commitment, using his family ties to achieve postings to active conflicts in preference to languishing in the less troubled parts of India.

To boost his own and his recently widowed mother's income, Churchill combined soldiering with writing and capitalised on each campaign in which he fought, nowhere more so than after escaping from captivity during the Boer War in 1899. His ambition was to emulate his father's success in politics and his hero's welcome on return to Britain helped propel him to a seat in Parliament as Conservative member for Oldham in 1900. His long journey to political fame had begun.

**Opposite** Winston in sailor suit, Dublin, aged five.
**Above left** 'Young Churchill' section of the museum.
**Above right** Poster in Afrikaans and English offering a £25 reward for information leading to Churchill's recapture.
**Below** Winston's baby rattle.

Churchill came to politics as though, literally, born to it, his father's reputation serving both to mark him out and mark him down. He advanced rapidly, gaining his first ministerial post in 1905, though only by joining the Liberal Party, with which he continued to serve, until 1924 when he returned to the Conservatives and a life-long mistrust within the party.

In 1908 he married the woman who was to be not only his partner for the rest of his life, but also his closest friend and confidante, Clementine Hozier. A committed Liberal, she supported him and stuck by him throughout his turbulent career.

It comes as a surprise to many people to learn that Churchill's Liberal years were marked by a series of measures and social reforms for which he was responsible and which later would become the foundations of the Welfare State. His ministerial career was often controversial, among the most famous episodes being his appearance, while Home Secretary, at the 'Siege of Sidney Street'. His appointment as First Lord of the Admiralty in 1911, though he revolutionised the Navy – at that time the symbol of British power – aggrieved many traditionalists and senior officers. He was hounded from office in 1915 when his typically ambitious plan to capture the Dardanelles in an effort to shorten the war, failed, incurring heavy casualties.

In despair at this sudden interruption of his seemingly unstoppable rise to the highest office, Churchill returned to service with the army and commanded a battalion on the Western Front, reinforcing a reputation for bravery, which characterised his life and career thereafter.

The lure of politics, however, was too great and he returned to England to resume his ministerial career, rising to become Conservative Chancellor of the Exchequer from 1924 to 1929. In this post Churchill exhibited his maverick style, returning Britain to the Gold Standard, virtually taking command of the press during the General Strike and also working assiduously for the rights of striking and poorly paid miners.

However, in the 1929 General Election the Conservatives were defeated and Churchill was out of office and rejected by subsequent Prime Ministers for the next ten years.

**Above View of the Churchill Museum.
Below 'Kat and 'Pug', pet names Churchill and Clementine gave each other.
Opposite Clementine and Winston at Hendon Aerodrome, 1914.**

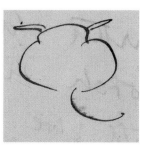

Maverick Politician

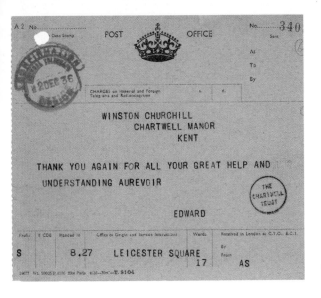

# 'I have always earned my living by my pen and my tongue'

**Winston Churchill**

This period of Churchill's life has unfairly become known as the 'wilderness years', simply because he held no ministerial post from 1929 to 1939. However, Churchill was a man of strong opinions and he never lacked a platform for their dissemination and did not attempt to conceal his views, regardless of public opinion. His support for King Edward VIII in the 1936 Abdication Crisis undoubtedly made the new King, George VI, and his consort distrustful of Churchill. His trenchant opposition to Indian independence in the 1930s won him few friends and further confirmed in many people's minds his lack of judgement. He aired his growing disagreement with the policy of appeasing Hitler with increasing vehemence, despite it being a government policy widely supported by the press and the public. His country home, Chartwell, in Kent, became a focus for those who did agree with him and supplied him with information, which he then used as the backbone of parliamentary arguments.

His principal means of making his views heard were also his principal means of earning a living: as a prolific writer of biographies, history books and articles on almost any subject, and as a much sought after speaker, in the United States and in Britain, although the BBC placed restrictions on him broadcasting.

As the hopes of the Munich agreement faded to a shameful recognition of a failed policy, Churchill's star once more began to rise. When war finally broke out in September 1939 the Prime Minister, Neville Chamberlain, had little choice but to invite Churchill to return to the government and appointed him to his old post of First Lord of the Admiralty. In this post he might have expected to be once more mired in the failure of a major military initiative – the Norway expedition – but the opprobrium fell almost wholly on the shoulders of Chamberlain who was then forced to resign. On 9 May, after days of politicking and intrigue, the favourite for the post of Prime Minister, Lord Halifax, ceded to Churchill whose appointment the King reluctantly agreed the next day. At last Winston was well and truly back and finally meeting what he long deemed to be his – and as it transpired his country's – destiny.

**Opposite** Churchill bricklaying at Chartwell in 1928.
**Above** Telegram from the Duke of Windsor thanking Churchill for his help and support. Churchill kept in touch with the King throughout the abdication crisis and helped to write his abdication speech.

"NEVER WAS SO MUCH OWED BY SO MANY TO SO FEW" *THE PRIME MINISTER*

The voice of Sir Winston Churchill is instantly recognisable. It is appropriate, therefore, that the first thing one encounters in the Churchill Museum is his voice, delivering phrases that have now entered the English language: 'Blood, toil, tears and sweat'; 'We shall fight on the beaches'; 'This was their finest hour'.

Churchill indeed 'mobilised the English language and sent it into battle' – a phrase used most famously by President John F Kennedy in his 1963 tribute to Churchill. In 1940, when Hitler's armies seemed poised to invade Britain, the nation's inspiration came from radio broadcasts of speeches by a man who, before the war, had been widely criticised for his opposition to the appeasement of Hitler and a lack of judgement over India and the Abdication. Though not everybody in the nation agreed with him, he was suddenly, and despite his privileged upbringing and tastes, both widely popular at home and, of course, mocked by the enemy. His personal habits – his appearance of being ready for action in his 'siren suit', his twice daily bath, afternoon nap and a penchant for cigars, champagne and other fine wines and food – never changed, despite the austerity of war, and indeed seemed to sustain his indefatigable constitution, while his wartime lifestyle exhausted those who served him.

**Opposite** Door to Number 10 Downing Street, which Churchill first walked through as Prime Minister in May 1940.
**Above left** Churchill inspecting Polish troops in Scotland.
**Above right** The stub of one of Churchill's Havana cigars. He would usually light his first cigar shortly after breakfast. He smoked about eight a day, constantly relighting and never inhaling them.
**Left** British poster inspired by Churchill's speech of 20 August 1940.

# 'There is only one thing worse than fighting with allies, and that is fighting without them'

Winston Churchill, 1940

**Opposite** Churchill in a pith helmet viewing the Alamein position, 7 August 1942.
**Left** Letter from King George VI pleading with Churchill not to be present at the D-Day landings, June 1944. Churchill agreed, very reluctantly.
**Below** 'War Leader' section of the museum.

The combative messages he delivered were translated into action as he took a firm and personal grip on government and military strategy, appointing himself Minister of Defence and emphasising the need for intelligence of the enemy's plans if victory was to be obtained.

Despite his constant reinforcement of a belief in victory, in his own mind he always knew that Britain could not win this battle alone or even with the support of its principal Allies at that time – in particular the British Commonwealth, France and the exiles of Nazi occupied Europe. He knew that American help and the entry of the United States into the war would be vital to victory and he put a great deal of his time and energy into courting President Roosevelt and the American people. He despised Communism all his life, but, as a realist, saw that the war would hinge on Russia's fate and immediately offered Britain's support when the Nazis invaded the Soviet Union in June 1941. With American entry into the war in December 1941, Churchill knew that eventual victory was assured.

To admirers of Winston Churchill it is difficult to understand how, in the General Election of 1945, an 'ungrateful nation' as he put it, could have cast him aside, after years of his inspirational leadership of his country in the war against Hitler.

Despite his defeat in the July 1945 election, the country, indeed the world, recognised in Winston Churchill a truly great figure and honours were heaped upon him at home and from abroad. Dejected by his failure with the electorate, he turned once again to his old hobby, painting, which he had begun as therapy after his rejection in 1915 following the Dardanelles debacle. Much of his prolific painting output dates from the post-war years, from regular visits to France, Morocco and the United States and while enjoying the hospitality of wealthy friends such as Aristotle Onassis. He also enjoyed some success as a racehorse owner.

Churchill remained Leader of the Conservative Party and a Member of Parliament, but felt free to take up again his principle source of income: writing. His multi-volume works *The Second World War* and *A History of the English-Speaking Peoples* enjoyed international success. In 1953, his published oeuvre earned him the Nobel Prize for Literature. He had shown that, despite his advancing years and being out of government, he could still shake the world with his words. In his 'iron curtain' speech, delivered at Fulton, Missouri, on 5 March 1946, he alerted the post-war world to the peril of Communism, in words that became a byword for the Cold War in the English language.

When the nation finally returned Churchill to power in 1951 at the age of 76, he continued to emphasise the threat of a nuclear war between the West and the Soviet Union. He was an ardent believer in 'jaw jaw' in preference to 'war war' and a strong advocate of 'summit' meetings of world leaders. Though the Super Powers never agreed to any such meetings during his period as Prime Minister, his ideas eventually became the accepted norm of international power politics.

He continued to serve as a Member of Parliament until six months before his death at the age of 90, but his final years were increasingly marked more by his absence from, rather than his presence in, the House of Commons. After he died on 24 January 1965, Her Majesty Queen Elizabeth II gave him a State Funeral, which was broadcast around the world, finally sealing his iconic status.

THE·SWEDISH·ACADEM
ON·THE·15TH·OCTOBE
1953·DECIDED·TO·AWAR
SIR·WINSTON·CHURCHILL·K
THE·NOBEL       PRICE·IN
LITERA-         TURE·O
1953·FOR        HIS·MA
TERY·OF         HISTOR
·CAL·AND·BIOGRAPHICA
DESCRIPTION·AND·FO
THE·RESPLENDENT·PO
WER·OF·SPEECH·WITH
WHICH·HE·PRESENTS·HIM
SELF·AS·A·DEFENDER
OF·HIGH·HUMAN·RIGHTS

# 'But I leave the past, and I leave the present. It is to the future that we must turn our gaze.'

**Winston Churchill**

Museums, like icebergs, have most of their content out of view where their value cannot be easily appreciated. Not at the Churchill Museum. Our solution to the problem of how to make publicly available a mass of material about Churchill's life from archives and stores is the Lifeline, a 15 metre long interactive table chronicling the life and times of Winston Churchill. The visitor can access 1,100 documents, 1,150 images and 10 films plus an almost unquantifiable abundance of written information, giving an opportunity to explore Churchill's life almost day by day. Letters that Churchill wrote to his mother can be found alongside his exchanges with Stalin and Roosevelt. To add excitement to the search for information, over 200 dates activate special animations and sounds: on Armistice Day, 11 November 1918, the whole table becomes a bed of red poppies; on another date Charles Lindbergh flies his plane the full length of the table, while in 1953, Churchill's Nobel Prize for literature suddenly makes an appearance. We continue to add to the software so that the Lifeline's content remains up-to-date and reflects the latest historical perspectives. The table is, in effect, a living biography of Churchill and a vibrant study of his era, embodying IWM's commitment to using cutting-edge technology, sophisticated design and fine scholarship to bring Churchill to life.

### Learning Department

Churchill War Rooms offers a range of options for schools, colleges, youth groups and adult group visitors.

UK and overseas schools and youth groups can explore the Cabinet War Rooms and Churchill Museum on a self-directed visit. UK schools may add a learning session to their itinerary during term time.

All visits must be pre-booked. Contact us via **learningbookings@iwm.org.uk** or visit **iwm.org.uk/churchill**

### Events

A diverse calendar of events takes place throughout the year, such as presentations of wartime films, interactive creative sessions for children of all ages and lectures. Please see our website for further information, **iwm.org.uk/churchill**

### Corporate Hospitality

Churchill War Rooms can be hired for corporate or private use and makes an ideal setting for business meetings, presentations, dinners, receptions, product launches and seminars. Air-cooled and boasting state of the art facilities, in a unique historic setting, rooms can accommodate from 10 to 450 people. For more information call us on 020 7766 0134 or e-mail **cwr@sodexo.com**

### We need your support

The Churchill Museum was achieved solely as a result of the generosity of many individuals, trusts and companies. We receive no direct government funding. To keep the museum open and to sustain the services associated with it costs over £3 million each year. This is in addition to the massive costs of preserving and making publicly accessible the historic Churchill War Rooms.

To help support this great museum you can donate in one of three ways

- online at **iwm.org.uk**

- by cheque made payable to Imperial War Museum, sent to Phil Reed, Director, Churchill War Rooms, Clive Steps, King Charles Street, London, SW1A 2AQ
  tel **020 7930 6961**
  e **preed@iwm.org.uk**

- US-based donors can give through a tax-efficient scheme. For details please contact the Director of Churchill War Rooms:
  Phil Reed, Director, Chuchill War Rooms, Clive Steps, King Charles Street, London, SW1A 6961
  tel **020 7930 6961**
  e **preed@iwm.org.uk**